The Revelation of the Dragon

Terryann Scott

No More Walls

The Revelation of the Dragon: No More Walls
Volume 1 of *"The 'No More' Series"*

Scripture quotations are from the King James Version of the Holy Bible (KJV).

© 2012 Terryann Scott

All rights reserved. No part of this book may be reproduced or transmitted in any form or by any means, electronically or mechanically, without permission in writing from the author.
Please note that specific nouns have not been capitalized, such as satan and other related counterparts. This is intentional as homage is not credited to such.

eBook Edition
ISBN: 978-976-95696-0-7
ASIN: B00LXG8M96

Print Edition
ISBN: 978-976-95696-1-4

Request for information should be addressed to:
info.scottspublishing@gmail.com

Cover Design by:
Danever Scott

BOOKS BY THIS AUTHOR

———

Becoming a Better You: Heal Your Soul; Heal Your Life
Keys to the Kingdom: Unlocking the Mystery of Prayer
The Revelation of the Dragon: No More Walls
Roads to Success: No More Barriers
Overcoming Obstacles: Hope Devotional
Surviving Challenging Times: Faith Devotional
Finding God: Love Devotional
Hidden Truths: Daily Devotional
Sixty-One Thoughts That Can Change Your Life: Wisdom Nuggets

*In honor of you, Lord.
To the Father, Son, and Holy Spirit.*

*This book is dedicated to
all the people who are struggling with oppression,
suppression, lack, fear, depression, health problems,
marital problems, anger, bitterness, unforgiveness
and absent-mindedness, among other things.*

*Dedicated to everyone who
sees or hears themself on these pages.*

PRAYER

Father, in the name of your Son Jesus Christ, I approach your throne now. I thank you for your love towards us, in that while we were yet sinners, you died for us. Thank you for the revelatory knowledge you have shown me concerning the spirit of the dragon.
As this information goes out, I pray that the eyes of your people will be opened, their minds freed, and their understanding enlightened. May lives be transformed, may hearts be blessed, and may their spirits be renewed. May empowerment be theirs now by the power of the Holy Spirit. I cancel and nullify every satanic backlash, in Jesus' name I pray, Amen.

CONTENTS

Acknowledgements	11
Foreword	13
Introduction	15
1. Spirits And Ranks	21
2. The Dragon Revealed	33
3. Are You Cursed?	45
4. Breaking Barriers	55
5. A Word Of Caution	77
6. Sample Prayer	93
Epilogue	101
Dear Readers	105
About the Author	107
Let's Connect	111
Books by Terryann Scott	113

ACKNOWLEDGEMENTS

I first want to recognize and thank the Godhead–Father, Son, and Holy Spirit- for the revelatory knowledge and inspiration to write this book. A special thank you goes to the Holy Spirit, my friend, for His guidance and direction.

I must thank my husband, Danever Scott, for all his input, motivation, and support during this process. Thanks for being my cheerleader through all of this, honey, and most importantly, thank you for being the man God has designed you to be. Truly, you are a man after God's Heart. I thank you for being a positive part of this transformation process and for designing the book's cover. May God continue to bless you, may He strengthen, uphold, and keep you. May He continue to embrace you into His fullness and give you His peace.

Thanks to Bishop Richard McKenzie for doing my

photo shoot and for all your support during the publication process.

Thanks to my mom, Aneita Brown, and my sister, Denisha Robinson, for your encouragement and support. I extend my appreciation to you, Denisha, for doing my makeup for the book's cover.

I must also recognize my children, Judah Scott and Kayla Scott. Thank you for putting up with me while I dedicated my time to writing.

Let me say a final thank you to all who encouraged and supported me during the production of this book. Special thanks also to those who have purchased a copy of this book or have shared information about buying it.

May God bless you all as you read this book.

FOREWORD

The Revelation of the Dragon is a powerful, truly inspiring book that is a must-have for all Christians and even for those curious about its contents. I have read many books on dragons throughout my fourteen (14) years of ministry; many of which, concerning style of writing and delivery of the content, were difficult to comprehend.

Minister Terryann Scott has written about the Dragon in a reader-friendly manner that captures the reader's interest from start to finish, forcing you to anxiously explore how to deal with "this beast" affecting your life.

The Revelation of the Dragon is a well-written book that offers hope to the reader. Terryann Scott is one of those unique people who have impacted my life tremendously in many ways, and this book has been another medium through which I have been affected.

---Richard McKenzie
Apostle, Bishop, Senior Pastor
Kingdom Life Worship Centre Ministries (KLWCM), Jamaica

Author of six books:
    200 *Important Things to Think About, A True Heart-Breaking Story about Hell, A Miraculous Recovery, The One in a Million Mom: From my Heart to Yours, A Touch of Blindness: Healed by God,* and *Embrace Your Suffering.*

INTRODUCTION

I was in the middle of a messy situation, and I grew tired and frustrated as almost everything in my life went wrong. I was never a sickly person, but at this particular time, I began to experience a series of illnesses like never before. Everything started going downhill, leading to one problem after another.

Things were a bit shaky before, but it all began in 2010 after giving birth to my second daughter, Kayla. I developed pregnancy-induced hypertension that would not subside without the use of daily high-dose pressure medication, and then came double pneumonia, which almost claimed my life just three weeks after giving birth. I also began to experience pain in my abdomen and severe pain in my back to the point where I had to get an injection at the hospital every week for the pain, as walking became difficult, tablets were useless, and the list went on.

I was challenged with battling health problems, financial problems, marital problems, and other issues. This frustration drove me to a sincere search for God. I was a Christian for many years, but my struggles forced me to seek God more in a heartfelt way.

I was certain there was a curse–or something close to a curse–over the family, so I started to seek God in this direction. I went on a series of fasting – thirteen days to be exact – as I discovered that 13 is the number for stubbornness and rebellion according to biblical numerology, and I was desperate for my stubborn situation to change.

I noticed during the fast that I was not only drawing closer to God, but that God was drawing closer to me. My spiritual life was revamped, and I was now on a mission to seek God for who He is. I felt such closeness after crying out to God in all my pain and from the desperation of my heart, and I was discovering Him!

This tangible presence of God became my focus, as it quenched the thirst and longing in my soul. I was finding my way in the presence of God, and this awareness aroused me to become adamant about not entertaining anything in my life that was not of God, such as sickness, lack–you name it. Two years before I began my journey, my husband had an encounter with God that prompted him to ensure his love life aligned with the fruits of Love, as described in 1 Corinthians 13.

INTRODUCTION

There, his radical journey with God began stemming from marital issues. I was now just starting my journey after having my encounter, and I was loving it. As I sought God to reveal everything in or over our lives that needed to be broken, I began to hear the words "swallow up." It was as though I was recalling something previously said, so I made inquiries.

Sure enough, the replies were vague, so I started to question God about the words instead. As I petitioned the Lord, I felt the Holy Spirit's call to seek God more in prayer.

Prayer was difficult for me. I prayed yes, but I could not find the time to pray as I wanted, as I was faced with the responsibility of caring for our two young children, which was a significant distraction, especially when it came to prayer. I appreciate my sleep at night, and if I do not defend anything else, I most certainly know how to protect my sleep. Still, the pull I felt to seek God was more than I could explain, so much so that I decided to sacrifice time at night to pray, as I was unable to do so effectively during the day.

After making my decision, I lay in bed one night to pray. As I closed my eyes, I saw a close-up view of part of an animal. The skin had a basketball-like texture, with spots. I remember seeing a smooth, cream-colored texture, which led me to believe I was seeing the belly (or the side of the belly) of a beast. Even though I saw no wings, I somehow knew that the creature had wings. I immediately opened my eyes and began asking the Lord what He was showing me. I got no answer, so I prayed, then I fell asleep.

While I was sleeping, I dreamt that I was in a strange place and the spirit of fear wanted to attack me. I could not see this spirit, but I could feel its presence, and I knew it would attack me. Though I was in a strange place, I was familiar with the surroundings, so I made my way to the bathroom for a shower.

As I started to shower, the spirit of fear jumped on me, attaching itself to my entire face using its claws. The location in the dream had now changed, and I was talking to a sister of mine who said, "When trouble comes, I dive under Psalm 91." I responded that I love using Psalm 23 in times of trouble, but in the dream, I did not have any special scripture I loved, so I was uncertain why I said that. I awoke from the dream, and I brought it immediately before the Lord.

I almost fell asleep again when I literally felt the hand of God grab my spirit and raise it partly out of my body. As the Lord took hold of my spirit, I heard the words spoken into my spirit (yes, it felt like my spirit had its own ears): "break the claws of the enemy and pluck its scales out." Before my spirit was released, He continued, "You really need to find time in the nights to pray because it is in the nights that this spirit gains its strength." I woke up as my spirit was released back into my body.

INTRODUCTION

After some serious deliberation with myself and the Lord, I knew that I was still in my right mind and without doubt God was trying to tell me something, but what?

The following day after church, I sat on the bed to relax, but the questions, 'What could that be? What was the Lord showing me and what is He trying to tell me?' kept flooding my mind. Suddenly, without warning, my spirit came alive, and the surroundings gave way as the words or knowledge travelled straight into my spirit and lodged there. Immediately, I raised myself from off the bed and exclaimed, "Oh my God, it's a dragon! It's a dragon!" as the revelation hit home.

A few days after my experience, I decided to search the internet for images of a dragon. I was startled at the results. The first link that I clicked on revealed the exact creature that I saw. The color and skin texture were the same, and after a close examination of the picture, the texture appeared scale-free (just like what I saw), but it still had scales! I knew for sure that God was telling me something.

As my eagerness grew, I remembered Psalm 91, which had been mentioned in my dream, so I grabbed my Bible and began reading it. As I read verse 13, I was amazed to find the word *dragon* in it! I was astonished! I knew without doubt that God was revealing something, so I decided to study the Bible on the subject to see what the scriptures had to say about this beast. I knew it was a demonic spirit, but I wanted to know more: what kind of spirit it was, what role it plays, how it affects people's lives... everything. I was enthused with what I had discovered.

1
SPIRITS AND RANKS

We need to realize that demons are real. Demons do exist. One way the devil fights a Christian Believer or any other person is by blinding him or her from the truth to keep them in ignorance. The devil knows and understands that if he can keep people in ignorance, he can destroy them.

> *"My people are destroyed for lack of knowledge: because thou hast rejected knowledge, I will also reject thee, that thou shalt be no priest to me: seeing thou hast forgotten the law of thy God, I will also forget thy children"* (Hosea 4:6).

It is a serious thing to remain ignorant of God's Word because ignorance leads to destruction. The devil's mission here on earth is to destroy.

> *"The thief cometh not, but for to steal, and to kill, and to destroy: I am come that they might have life, and that they might have it more abundantly"* (St. John 10:10).

> *"And the Lord said, Simon, Simon, behold, Satan hath desired to have you, that he may sift you as wheat"* (St. Luke 22:31).

> *"Be sober, be vigilant; because your adversary the devil, as a roaring lion, walketh about, seeking whom he may devour"* (1 Peter 5:8).

To accomplish this mission, the devil has made for himself an organized army of demons that will work to destroy us at all costs.

This army comprises different sectors, with the most powerful spirits serving as heads of each category. These head-spirits are referred to as king demons/spirits, but I prefer to call them ruling spirits or principalities. The terms can be used interchangeably as a King rules and a Ruler rules, even though there are minor differences.

Other Ministers and Authors may refer to these spirits by different names, but the functions usually remain the same.

The weaker spirits carry out instructions given by king spirits, and demons are disciplined enough to get the task done—more disciplined than some Christians. No wonder the state we are in.

Revelation chapters 13, 16, and 20 tell us about the dragon.

> *"And the beast which I saw was like unto a leopard, and his feet were as the feet of a bear, and his mouth as the mouth of a lion: and the dragon gave him his power, and his seat, and great authority.*
>
> *And they worshipped the dragon which gave power unto the beast: and they worshipped the beast, saying, who is like unto the beast? Who is able to make war with him?*
>
> *And I beheld another beast coming up out of the earth; and he had two horns like a lamb, and he spake as a dragon"* (Revelation 13: 2, 4, 11).
>
> *"And the sixth angel poured out his vial upon the great river Euphrates; and the water thereof was dried up, that the way of the kings of the east might be prepared.*
>
> *And I saw three unclean spirits like frogs come out of the mouth of the dragon, and out of the mouth of the beast, and out of the mouth of the false prophet.*

> *For they are the spirits of devils, working miracles, which go forth unto the kings of the earth and of the whole world, to gather them to the battle of that great day of God Almighty"* (Revelation 16:12-14).

> *"And he laid hold on the dragon, that old serpent, which is the Devil, and Satan, and bound him a thousand years"* (Revelation 20:2).

I need to note that the dragon in the book of Revelation refers to the devil and is distinct from the dragon I'll be discussing in this book, which is a powerful head demon.

The first thing that came to my mind after receiving insight from the Holy Spirit into this matter was the question, Did dragons really exist? This subject may be controversial because studies and scientific research have yet to prove its existence, as there are no fossil or skeletal remains of this creature to work with (the lizard family with the term dragon at the end of its name differs). Some have concluded that this is a mythical creature, implying that the dragon is just a fairy tale, but we who are spiritual should know that this is more than just a fairy tale.

The fact that the Bible speaks of the dragon tells us that dragons do exist, but in the spiritual realm; therefore, they are demonic spirits.

When this reality hit me, I asked myself: how could someone have awareness of what this spirit being looks like if it exists only in the spiritual realm? This was a rhetorical question as I already knew the answer, but I was just enlightened.

There are persons in witchcraft (including satanism and other cult movements) who work along with spirits, and these persons are aware of the forms that these demonic spirits take. Persons who indulge in witchcraft also have professions and various positions that grant them access to get information out in whatever form they desire. The media is the best and most common medium in which persons involved in witchcraft will try to create ideas to deceive people into thinking that these images are 'mere' expressions or just creative imagination.

How many times have we watched a cartoon or a movie with a dragon in it, and we allowed ourselves to be entertained? How many times have we allowed our children to watch cartoons with unicorns in them, and we made nothing of it? How many times have we watched other movies and cartoons with strange-looking characters or creatures, and we gave no thought to it? We have allowed ourselves to become entertained by the images of these demonic spirits regularly and fail to realize it.

In cartoons and movies, the dragon depicts what it is good at doing–holding people hostage, sometimes in chains and in dungeons. Does that sound familiar–Dungeons and Dragons? A highly demonic board game used by people dabbling in the occult. This explains why we are having so many problems in our lives. This explains why our children are so stubborn and rebellious, and why parents wonder what is wrong with them when we are the ones to blame. We have allowed them to open their spirits to demonic influences.

The clothing we wear creates another problem. Christians are purchasing brands and labels that are owned and cursed by satanists. Whenever our children or we wear these, we attract curses to ourselves and to our children. Christians also get caught up in traditional activities and celebrations that are explicitly geared towards the celebration of the devil, such as Halloween. The very meaning of Halloween–a celebration of the dead–should tell us this is no celebration for Christians. Many of the Halloween costumes also confirm this. I pray the Christian community will wake up and begin to allow God to lead. If we do not stop in our tracks and begin to seek God, our lives will be at stake.

Be careful what you watch, be careful what you read, be careful what you wear, be careful what you listen to, be careful what you do, and be careful where you go.

There are two types of dragons: one that has wings that breathe or spits fire from its mouth, and another in the form of a serpent without wings (looks similar to a sea horse in my opinion). Remember, I do not speak of the lizard family that exists in reality.

This is a spirit known to be very powerful, and when

used in witchcraft, it is called upon and sought after for its power. They appear in different colors: red, blue, gold, and so on, each of which signifies something different, but they all point and lead to power (we will not discuss that here).

> *"And the wild beasts of the islands shall cry in their desolate houses, and dragons in their pleasant palaces: and her time is near to come, and her days shall not be prolonged"* (Isaiah 13:22).

> *"In that day the Lord with his sore and great and strong sword shall punish leviathan the piercing serpent, even leviathan that crooked serpent; and he shall slay the dragon that is in the sea"* (Isaiah 27:1).

Isaiah 13, 27, and Revelation 20:2 indicate that the dragon spirit is a King demon or a Ruling spirit. Only a king or a ruler rules over a particular set of people. The scripture also tells us that this creature dwells in its pleasant palaces, which suggests ownership; therefore, it would be a King. The fact that the dragon is likened unto the devil and holds the same title given to the devil shows the authority and rank that comes with this spirit, the dragon. It is one of the highest-ranking spirits and holds such power that it becomes obvious it is a King demon, or in other words, a Ruling spirit.

In all my studies and research, the spirit of the Dragon is one of the most powerful demons I have encountered, as are the spirits of Leviathan and Behemoth. The dragon is a powerful spirit controlling the lives of many people right now, and they are not even aware of it.

The Bible speaks in detail about the spirit of leviathan in Job 41. You can make time to read all of it, but a part of it says:

> "His scales are his pride, shut up together as with a close seal. One is so near to another that no air can come between them. They are joined one to another; they stick together, that they cannot be sundered. By his sneezing a light doth shine, and his eyes are like the eyelids of the morning. Out of his mouth go burning lamps, and sparks of fire leap out. Out of his nostrils goeth smoke, as out of a seething pot or caldron. His breath kindleth coals, and a flame goeth out of his mouth. In his neck remaineth strength, and sorrow is turned into joy before him. The flakes of his flesh are joined together: they are firm in themselves; they cannot be moved. His heart is as firm as a stone; yea, as hard as a piece of the nether millstone. When he raiseth up himself, the mighty are afraid: by reason of breakings they purify themselves. The sword of him that layeth at him cannot hold: the spear, the dart, nor the habergeon.

He esteemeth iron as straw, and brass as rotten wood. The arrow cannot make him flee: sling stones are turned with him into stubble. Darts are counted as stubble: he laugheth at the shaking of a spear. Sharp stones are under him: he spreadeth sharp pointed things upon the mire. He maketh the deep to boil like a pot: he maketh the sea like a pot of ointment. He maketh a path to shine after him; one would think the deep to be hoary. Upon earth there is not his like, who is made without fear. He beholdeth all high things: he is a king over all the children of pride."

We can clearly see in the last verse that Leviathan is a king demon, ruling those with pride. This spirit is the driving force behind those with pride, and under this particular type of spirit comes the spirit of misunderstandings, strife, and so much more.

I need people to understand the power behind these spirits, as Job states, *"Iron is as straw before him and brass as rotten wood."* The scripture says that, *"Arrows cannot make him flee; he laughs at the shaking of a spear. Sorrow is turned into joy before him,"* and the question was asked in verses not mentioned above, *"Who will be able to stand before me? None is so fierce to stir him up,"* the Word says. This is no joke. Ministers have to be very careful when confronting these spirits.

The anointing and guidance of the Holy Spirit are crucial. A lot of people, Christians alike, are under the influence or control of demons in some way. I need to highlight that one does not have to be possessed by demons before they operate under the influence of demons. Demons operate from without and within their target, causing oppression and possession. These spirits can create walls in our lives and hinder us from the blessings of God (suppression). Fear, anxiety, worry, doubt, anger, bitterness, hatred, unforgiveness, confusion, and much more are spirits that manifest in our lives at times. If we are not careful, they can gain control and become strongholds in our lives.

Anything that is taking you over or anything that has control of you will become a stronghold and is oppression. So, if you find that you are having difficulty keeping your anger under control, for example, and you are always getting upset sometimes for simple reasons, it could mean that the spirit of anger is in operation and has a stronghold in your life.

The Bible says we are to be angry and sin not, so we know that we can be angry and not sin, but whenever you find things getting out of hand to the degree where you cannot help but to become angry, or you can't help but to worry–even when things are going good–once you are having difficulty to gain control of yourself, this is worth looking into.

> *"For where envying and strife is, there is confusion and <u>every evil work</u>"* (James 3:16). Note phrase underlined.

Anything that controls you or your life is a stronghold. Strongholds act like walls in our lives. We cannot get past these walls until they are dealt with. These walls can hinder what God has in store for us and block us from our destiny. It is the devil's plan for us to operate within walls, as this act of confinement literally holds us in sin as we operate outside of faith and in disobedience. The devil can only touch us if he has legal access to us, and sin gives him legal rights to touch us, as we are no longer under the covering of Jesus Christ when we sin, except we repent. God honors true repentance, and His grace and mercy are sufficient to keep us. As children of God, it is our responsibility to ensure that we live a righteous life before God in obedience so that the devil will not be able to accuse us.

Other types of common strongholds are: stubbornness, rebellion, alcoholism, sex, drugs, rage, pride, adultery, fornication, low self-esteem, wrong mindsets, the need to always be in control, defensiveness, and so on.

If there are walls in your life, it is not of God. Walls create limitations, and it was never God's intention for us to live a limited or defeated life. If you identify any strongholds in your life, acknowledge them, confess them, and ask God for His forgiveness, healing, and strength to face and resist these spirits daily. This is the only way to overcome. We must put up a fight to resist.

> *"Submit yourselves therefore to God. Resist the devil, and he will flee from you"* (James 4:7).

2
THE DRAGON REVEALED

I f God is God, serve Him.

After studying a few scripture passages about the dragon, I have learnt to identify traits that depict the workings of this spirit in someone's marriage, home, ministry, business/organization, or life as a whole.

> "And thorns shall come up in her palaces, nettles and brambles in the fortresses thereof: and it shall be a habitation of dragons, and a court for owls" (Isaiah 34:13).

> "And I will make Jerusalem heaps, and a den of dragons; and I will make the cities of Judah desolate, without an inhabitant" (Jeremiah 9:11).

> *"Nebuchadnezzar the king of Babylon hath devoured me, he hath crushed me, he hath made me an empty vessel, he hath swallowed me up like a dragon, he hath filled his belly with my delicates, he hath cast me out"* (Jeremiah 51:34).

> *"And I hated Esau, and laid his mountains and his heritage waste for the dragons of the wilderness"* (Malachi 1:3).

The passages you have just read may seem confusing to you, but they are very clear and informative if you reread and acquire an understanding through the help of the Holy Spirit.

> *"But the natural man receiveth not the things of the Spirit of God: for they are foolishness unto him: neither can he know them, because they are spiritually discerned"* (2 Corinthians 2:14).

To help you understand, I will highlight a few keywords from the passages just read. They are: desolate, devoured, crushed, empty, swallowed, waste, and the phrase, cast out.

These are the works of the dragon or some of the results of the dragon at work. Do you have an idea where I'm going now?

Anywhere that lacks, barrenness, emptiness, unfruitfulness, poverty, desolation, or destruction is, the working of the dragon is suspected.

The type of lack, barrenness, emptiness, and so on, which is associated with this type of spirit, is distinctive. Let's look at an example.

Jane has a good-paying job, but at the end of each month, she finds herself in debt even after budgeting wisely. No matter what she does, critical expenses keep emerging, preventing her from getting out of debt, no matter how hard she tries.

This is a typical pattern of the dragon spirit invading her life. Keep in mind that when she spends, she does so wisely and not unnecessarily, but external situations caused by this spirit leave her with no choice but to meet unexpected demands. Instead of Jane living an everyday, comfortable life that her income can afford, she ends up in debt.

Let's look at another example.

Mike is a young, ambitious man who is hardworking. He has many business ideas that could improve his business and boost income, but each time he sets out to implement them, something comes up that forces him to delay his plans. Sometimes he may complain about weariness or extreme fatigue–whatever the case, there is always something valid that hinders him from making progress. Every time he attempts to go against the odds by pushing through the fatigue or whatever he is challenged with, he ends up losing opportunities that were given to him.

Please take note that each time Mike sets out to do something to improve his business and his income, the effects of the dragon spirit are manifested. In this scenario, it manifested as unusual fatigue and missed opportunities whenever he pushed through the exhaustion, as the aim of this spirit is to keep its victim in a dry, barren state.

Sometimes we set out to accomplish goals or make a radical move that will bring a radical change to our lives, and we, too, begin to experience unexplained fatigue, severe discouragement, or frustration. These are all traits of the dragon spirit operating in our lives, hindering our progression.

If we read and carefully study the scripture passages mentioned earlier, we will discover that this spirit brings with it affliction, suppression, oppression, frustration, suffering, fear, torment, bondage, hopelessness, sadness, distress, and sickness. These are all secondary effects, as shown in the examples above.

Let me share another example using myself. In my late teenage years, my family started having trouble with the water system in our house. Each time we installed new washers, we needed another soon after. When a washer was not required, we had to change the entire basin faucet. Even after the faucet was replaced, the pipe started leaking again, to the point that we had to use the outside lock-off after each use. As if that was not frustrating enough, one of the pipes failed, and that sink could no longer be used until the pipe was fixed or replaced. We decided not to spend any more money unnecessarily, as we had plans to abandon that section of the house for remodeling.

A new section of the house was built, new pipes installed, and we began to experience the same problem on the new side! This went on for years! Each time we got the pipes fixed, they went bad again; hence, my quest to seek God concerning some long-standing issues in my life. I knew it was not normal. It was as though something wanted us to live in a defeated state, and I realize now that it was the dragon spirit in operation in our lives.

Jeremiah described his experience as a 'swallow up' experience, and that is what this spirit sets out to do: steal and rob us of our blessings. The dragon is known for its keen eyesight, and it can spot our blessings before we even see them coming. Of course, the dragon not only spots our blessings, but it swallows them up before they get to us.

Have you ever been promised a job, some money, a house, or any other thing that is beneficial to you, and you were certain of that promise until something unexpected happened, causing you to miss that blessing or opportunity? We've had way too many of those.

I remember one instance when my mother's car, which the family used, was stolen. My husband and I had to hire a taxi every day to take us to work and wherever our feet could not take us. It was very costly, both in time and money. It wasn't easy. A particular person saw our situation and decided to give my husband a car. He showed us the car that would have been ours after he first sold a piece of land to purchase a new vehicle for himself. It was a lovely four-door Honda in excellent condition.

We were happy, excited, and grateful to God for such a blessing. The entire process was going to take approximately three months, and we were bursting with joy. About a month later, the gentleman told us he was experiencing difficulty selling his land. He already had the buyer, and the sale was certain, but all of a sudden, the deal fell through, and we missed the opportunity.

I recall another instance with a particular group that wanted to record with my husband, and they promised to pay us a certain amount the following week. We were happy about that because the majority of our customers do business with us on a payment plan, but this group was going to make a good portion of the payment at once, and we were delighted.

The week they promised to make payment, we received a call that payment would not be possible due to an accident they had while driving, which resulted in a little boy's foot being broken. The money that should have been ours had to be used to cover the expenses from that accident.

These are all examples of satanic swallowing; the working of the dragon in our lives. This became a trend for a particular season. I recall again another person who was on their way to us to make a payment, and their child got sick, which forced them to divert to the hospital, and the money got used on the child. Another client was heading our way to make a payment when their child suddenly became possessed by a demon. Another was on their way to make a payment, got stopped by the police, their car was seized, and you've guessed it–the money used to pay wrecking fees, and the stories could go on. Situations like these are not typical. It reveals a deliberate act by the devil against our lives.

These situations reflect or produce drought and dryness, which is associated with this spirit.

> *"And the parched ground shall become a pool, and the thirsty land springs of water: in the habitation of dragons, where each lay, shall be grass with reeds and rushes"* (Isaiah 35:7).

> *"The beast of the field shall honour me, the dragons and the owls: because I give waters in the wilderness, and rivers in the desert, to give drink to my people, my chosen"* (Isaiah 43:20).

This passage refers to the restoration of God's people

from this spirit. It also shows God's power over the dragon. It is God's will for us to be blessed. It is not His will for us to suffer lack, barrenness, or embarrassment. Our land should be blessed, our ground fruitful, our lives productive, and His people satisfied. This is a promise from God to us, and if we remain faithful to Him, it will come to pass in our lives.

> *"If ye be willing and obedient, ye shall eat the good of the land"* (Isaiah 1:19):

> *"Having therefore these promises, dearly beloved, let us cleanse ourselves from all filthiness of the flesh and spirit, perfecting holiness in the fear of God"* (2 Corinthians 7:1).

> *"Who through faith subdued kingdoms, wrought righteousness, obtained promises, stopped the mouths of lions"* (Hebrews 11:33).

Note carefully that other creatures or beasts are associated with the presence of the dragon. Isaiah mentions the lion, owl, wild beasts, ravenous beast, doleful creatures, vultures, and more in the same book. Let's take a look.

THE DRAGON REVEALED

"But wild beast of the desert shall lie there; and their houses shall be full of doleful creatures; and owls shall dwell there, and satyrs shall dance there. And the wild beast of the islands shall cry in their desolate houses and dragons in their pleasant palaces; and her time is near to come, and her days shall not be prolonged" (Isaiah 13:21-22).

"But the cormorant and the bittern shall possess it; the owl also and the raven shall dwell in it; and he shall stretch out upon it the line of confusion, and the stones of emptiness. And thorns shall come up in her palaces, nettles and brambles in the fortresses thereof: and it shall be a habitation of dragons, and a court for owls. The wild beast of the desert shall also meet with the wild beast of the island, and satyr shall cry to his fellow; the screech owl also shall rest there, and find for herself a place of rest. There shall the great owl make her nest, and lay, and hatch, and gather under her shadow: there shall the vultures also be gathered, everyone with her mate" (Isaiah 34: 11, 13-15).

"No lion shall be there, nor any ravenous beast shall go up there on, it shall not be found there; but the redeemed shall walk there" (Isaiah 35:9).

I want to define a few terms to clarify your understanding better.

DOLEFUL: Unhappy, mournful.
SATYRS: In Greek mythology, a woodland creature depicted as having the pointed ears, legs, and short horns of a goat and a fondness for unrestrained revelry, lecher, which means insatiable, impossible to satisfy.
CORMORANT: large fish-eating seabird, known for its voracity. Voracity means eating or wanting a lot of food.
BITTERN: small heron. A heron is a large, long-legged bird of rivers and lakes.
SCREECH OWL: owl with a harsh, shrill cry. Shrill means a high, painful, sharp sound.
RAVENOUS: very hungry.

Now reread the passages with the meaning of the explained terms in mind.

Can you see the heavy sorrow, oppression, and bondage involved? No wonder perplexity becomes a natural reaction to the prolonged stripping, emptiness, and lack that we face in our lives. This is one reason we may not prosper as God intends. It is not that provision has not been made, but ravenous predators await it, and most people are blind and oblivious to the fact that something is eating our blessings. An unseen battle is taking place. May God help us!

There is something significant I'd like to highlight from the scripture, and it is this. Any part of our lives that is not fully surrendered to God is left vulnerable to the enemy's attacks (read the entire passage of scriptures mentioned at the start of this chapter). God hates sin, and sin is the leading cause for this spirit to invade our lives. It is imperative to serve God and not play around if we choose to live for Him. God wants all of us and not just a part. Having one foot in and one foot out will, in no doubt, attract problems as sin gives the devil legal rights to touch us.

Please remember that adultery, fornication, murder, etc., are no different from worry, anxiety, fear, and so on, when it comes to sin. There is no sin that is bigger than the other in God's eyes. Sin is sin. If there is anything at all before you that you know you need to get rid of as a Child of God, do it now. Whatever you are not aware of, ask the Lord to reveal it to you so that you can repent. Do not allow ignorance to destroy you. God is speaking to you now. Listen to His voice and surrender your life completely to Him. Change what needs to be changed and allow God to help you to fix what needs to be fixed. This includes breaking strongholds, as strongholds are sinful barriers that block us from accessing what God has for us.

> *"Our heart is not turned back; neither have our steps declined from thy way; though thou hast sore*

> *broken us in the place of dragons, and covered us with the shadow of death. If we have forgotten the name of our God, or stretched out our hands to a strange god, shall not God search this out? For he knoweth the secrets of the heart"* (Psalm 44: 18-21).

The dragon spirit will invade our lives if we choose to live carelessly before God. Our disobedience will give the enemy legal access to our lives. Read Deuteronomy 28 to see a detailed list of curses that will come on us because of disobedience.

> *"For the earth which drinketh in the rain that cometh oft upon it, and bringeth forth herbs meet for them by whom it is dressed, receiveth blessing from God: But that which beareth thorns and briers is rejected, and is nigh unto cursing; whose end is to be burned"* (Hebrews 6:7-8).

3

ARE YOU CURSED?

A ccording to the American Dictionary, a curse is the source or cause of evil; to bring evil upon. In simple terms, a curse is the opposite of a blessing. The term evil refers to something that causes or is a source of suffering, injury, or destruction; wickedness.

There are different types of curses and various reasons why one may be cursed. Curses may appear in multiple forms and in other areas of one's life. In this chapter, we will explore three types of curses, a few forms of curses, and their effects.

Let's begin.

TYPES OF CURSES

The first type of curse I'll talk about is what I'll refer to as a <u>*GOD-INDUCED CURSE*</u>. This curse, as its name clearly states, is one sent by God. The scripture speaks of several instances in which God placed a curse or curses on someone or a particular group of people (e.g., Genesis 3). It is not God's desire to curse us, and He has therefore warned us of things we should not do to avoid curses. Christians need to understand that when we violate the laws of God or disobey His Word, we become vulnerable and open to curses. It is the grace of God that is keeping many of us, and our lives are not worse than they could have been. For every sin, there is a consequence, and for every sin, there is a punishment. The Word of God tells us that no sin goes unpunished, and this does not mean we will be punished only when God returns for us; we will feel the effects in our lives during this lifetime.

One reason we have so many setbacks and hardships in our lives is disobedience, which, in essence, is sin. Deuteronomy 28 speaks of the commands God gives us for our blessing, and He also warns us in the latter part of the same chapter about curses that will affect us if we do not keep or obey His commands. This is simple; if we do not want to attract curses to our lives, we must abide by God's Word and refrain from sin. Failure to comply can result in a curse.

Right now, we are living under a curse because of Adam and Eve's sin. Even the devil is cursed by God for this. The scripture declares that the woman will conceive in pain and by the sweat of a man's face we shall eat. This is a curse, but the cross makes a difference in the Believer's lives. Thank God for His mercy, which endures forever. Here is a portion of Genesis 3.

> *"And the Lord God said unto the serpent, Because thou hast done this, thou art cursed above all cattle, and above every beast of the field; upon thy belly shalt thou go, and dust shalt thou eat all the days of thy life:*
>
> *And I will put enmity between thee and the woman, and between thy seed and her seed; it shall bruise thy head, and thou shalt bruise his heel.*
>
> *Unto the woman he said, I will greatly multiply thy sorrow and thy conception; in sorrow thou shalt bring forth children; and thy desire shall be to thy husband, and he shall rule over thee.*
>
> *And unto Adam he said, Because thou hast hearkened unto the voice of thy wife, and hast eaten of the tree, of which I commanded thee, saying,*
>
> *Thou shalt not eat of it: cursed is the ground for thy sake; in sorrow shalt thou eat of it all the days of thy life;*

> *Thorns also and thistles shall it bring forth to thee; and thou shalt eat the herb of the field;*
>
> *In the sweat of thy face shalt thou eat bread, till thou return unto the ground; for out of it wast thou taken: for dust thou art, and unto dust shalt thou return."*

Did you see the imaginary picture painted of the intense war between God and the devil, and demonic spirits, and us? There is a fierce race going on even now as you read between good and evil; a brutal battle for our souls. Praise the Lord, we were placed above the devil when that new order was established (see verse 15). What a victorious position to be in.

The second type of curse I'll mention is the <u>SPEECH CURSE</u> (curse by speech). This curse happens intentionally and unintentionally, knowingly and unknowingly. Many people fail to realize that there is power in the spoken word. The heavens and the earth and every living thing that was created were created by the spoken Word of God, except for man. God took time to form humans in His own image from the dust of the ground. We are very special to Him.

The Bible tells us that *death and power lie within the tongue.* We have to be careful what we speak about the lives of our children, our loved ones, and others. Words can help to build a person or break a person. Sometimes people may speak over our lives or other people's lives ignorantly, not knowing the damage that can be done, but others mean what they say and say what they mean. This happens daily, and many times we are not even aware of what is said about us or spoken over our lives, or of the consequences that come with it. Words linger in the atmosphere, and the devil will always try to use those words against us to create problems.

Do not mistake God's mercies and intervention for powerlessness. A negative word spoken may not manifest in our lives as reality, but it can manifest as struggles, problems, and unnecessary pain. Have you ever heard anyone say, 'I can't do this' or 'I can't do that because my mother said I cannot do it?' How many times have you seen young people turn out to be nothing because they were told they would become nothing, and they believed those lies? I have seen young ladies who have no value for themselves because they were rejected, and they chose to believe they are worthless. Words hurt, words live on; words affect change—whether negative or positive—because words have power.

Our beliefs will determine the extent to which negative words spoken can affect our lives. Even then, when we are strong enough to counteract negativity or when we are unaware of what was spoken, we will still face unnecessary struggles, as spirits will try to invade our lives to bring those negative words to pass. We must understand that we are creative beings. We were made in the image and likeness of God, and just as God created the world with His Word (the worlds were framed by the Word of God-Hebrews 11:3), we too are given power to affect change in the atmosphere, and that is why the scripture tells us death and life are in the power of the tongue. We are creative beings with power by God's design. It is a good thing to pray each morning and to pull down every negative word that was spoken over your life, even those you are unaware of. Nullify and render those negative words powerless and declare that they will take no effect in your life in Jesus' name.

While it is essential to recognize the power of spoken words, do remember that thoughts have power too. We attract what we think; it was my negative thinking that got me into the dilemma I shared at the beginning of this book, so if you are in the habit of unhealthy thinking, you need to address it. I attracted sickness to myself with my thoughts, and it manifested in my body in various forms.

Do not forget, likewise, that you can curse yourself with your own words, thoughts, and beliefs. If you identify problems that were created by the misuse of words, check your belief system, address the issue, and break its power over your life in Jesus' name.

The third and final type of curse I'll talk about is what I'll refer to as an <u>**EVIL CURSE.**</u> This is done by people who are evil and desire to see or intentionally cause harm or inflict pain upon another person. This is usually associated with hate towards another. This is manifested in various forms we will discuss now (please note that occult idols, images, objects, and symbols, etc., also attract spirits and curses, so be careful of what you own and keep within your possession).

FORMS OF CURSES

Curses come with supernatural powers or forms. Supernatural beings can carry them out through prayer, chant, ritual, spell, hex, witchcraft, magic, spoken words, voodoo, and so on.

THE EFFECTS OF A CURSE

First and foremost, I believe that a true child of God cannot be affected by any type or form of curse if they remain faithful to God. I do not mean that we will not be challenged; we are in a fight, but we have power over the enemy.

If you are a weak Believer and you lack an understanding of God's Word, or if you are not at the place where you should be in God, then your life is open, and you are in danger of being exposed to curses.

THE REVELATION OF THE DRAGON

> *"For the rod of the wicked shall not rest upon the lot of the righteous; lest the righteous put forth their hands unto iniquity"* (Psalm 125:3).

The effects of curses are numerous. Often it results in: a broken home, a broken marriage or family, poverty, sickness, pain, suffering, affliction, distress, insanity, other forms of mental disorders, infertility, and death, among a host of different things.

Note that curses can affect the bloodline and travel down from one generation to the next. The scripture talks about God visiting the sins of our fathers to the children unto the third and fourth generation (*see also Hosea 4:6 again at the beginning of chapter 1*). If curses are not identified and broken, they can be passed down from your parents to you, to your children, and to your children's children, and so on.

If your parents' marriage failed and you find that your marriage is struggling and heading in the same direction, you should be watchful, as that could be an indication of a curse coming down the bloodline, and the same goes for other situations. If your mother had you as a young teenager and you had your first child also as a young teenager, there could be a curse following your bloodline. If that curse is not broken, your teenage child may end up having a baby, also continuing the cycle.

I recall the story of a particular family. The entire male

line in that family never lived past a certain age. This was pretty unusual as the age mentioned was still youthful. There was a different situation where cancer took out part of a family over a period of time. These are not normal.

Again, two young ladies were struggling to conceive. It was not until the situation was brought before God and the curse was broken that these young ladies were able to give their husbands not one child but children in different instances.

We must be careful about how we accept sicknesses and ailments in our lives, such as diabetes and hypertension, as these, too, can be, but are not limited to, the result of a curse. Do not fall into the trap of believing that if one or both of your parents have diabetes, you too are bound to get it. Medical science can determine genetics and what you may be predisposed to, but God has the final say; cycles can be broken and bodies restored in Jesus' name. The cross makes a difference in the Believer's life. Do not accept it!

If there are stubborn situations in your life, if a particular pattern or cycle seems to be following you, if you are in violation of the Word of God and you are not where you need to be in Him, then you may be living under a curse.

Before any curse can be broken, you first need to be able to identify that you are in a position where you need to be delivered. This can be done with the help of the Holy

Spirit through sincere prayer and knowledge of the Word. Anywhere a curse is, an open door or sin is usually present. These openings or loopholes must be identified and addressed promptly.

Once these are identified, repent and confess your sins before God, ask for His forgiveness, identify the curse by name, call out the area(s) of your life that are affected by the curse, break it in Jesus' name, declare yourself loose & set freed by the power of God, believe that you are free & delivered, allow God to do a new redemptive work in your life and sin no more. It will take effort on your part to resist the divisiveness of the devil and not fall back into old habits, but you must resist. This is how you will maintain your deliverance (*more on this in the next chapter*).

> *"If my people, which are called by my name, shall humble themselves, and pray, and seek my face, and turn from their wicked ways; then will I hear from heaven, and will forgive their sin, and will heal their land"* (2 Chronicles 7:14).

> *"Afterward Jesus findeth him in the temple, and said unto him, Behold, thou art made whole: sin no more, lest a worse thing come unto thee"* (St. John 5:14).

4

BREAKING BARRIERS

The main thing I remember about myself as a little girl is an unusual sadness, driven by fear and characterized by shyness. The Bible says the eyes are the windows to the soul, and it is a proven truth. Every sadness and pain that lodged in my entire being was revealed through my eyes. People questioned the look in my eyes, but no one that I can remember was informed enough to realize that I was struck with deep sadness.

This sadness brought with it a quiet that stirred within me, which I mistook for a part of my personality for many years. I thought my temperament would never allow me to express my joys openly or freely, and that I was withdrawn, quiet, and shy.

I didn't really understand myself, and this may sound funny, but I never took the time out to understand myself (you need to take time out to understand yourself if you don't).

I was far from being my true self and never even realized it. The only thing I became aware of was that I was not free, but once again, I accepted this as a part of my 'shy' personality.

I was very unfriendly and mean. Harsh words became my best friend, and I could hardly help myself from being horrible. The irony was that I had a deep desire for love, but I would never allow anyone to get close to me. It was tough for me to trust people, and I expressed my fears by being harsh with others. I was stuck in my own world, a world that I helped the devil create for me unknowingly. Thinking all this was just me, I prayed earnestly to God for years, asking Him to help me become a nice person, but I could not help myself, or so I thought.

The reality of the matter is, I was in deep bondage and needed deliverance from the life of oppression to which I had become accustomed. I was trapped within myself by walls of fear, rejection, bitterness, sadness, unforgiveness, anger that grew into rage, and the list goes on. I was trapped and caged by the spirit of the dragon, and I was blind to all of this.

I began to deal radically with myself under my husband's counsel, and I experienced change. Still, after the Lord gave me this revelation about the spirit of the dragon, change became more rapid and apparent because I finally understood what was happening and what was required of me. For the first time in my life, I began to experience happiness as I discovered how to let go and give my all to God. At first, I was not aware of what happiness felt like until I realized what I was experiencing was indeed true happiness.

The peace of God, joy, and freedom you'll experience after being freed from the powers of darkness will eventually bring you so much happiness as you discover your true self. The dragon spirit is mighty, as mentioned before, but praise God, it is not more powerful than God who created it.

"Thou didst divide the sea by thy strength: thou breakest the heads of the dragons in the waters. Thou breakest the heads of Leviathan in pieces, and gavest him to be meat to the people inhabiting the wilderness" (Psalm 74:13-14).

"God hath spoken once; twice have I heard this; that power belongeth unto God" (Psalm 62:11).

Before I share the prayer points the Lord gave me concerning the spirit of the dragon, I would like to share something even more important with you: how to obtain and become transporters or carriers of the presence of God.

THE PRESENCE OF GOD

The presence of God is vital in the Believer's life because it is God's presence that protects and keeps us from all evil and harm. It is our duty as Children of God to seek God genuinely for more of Him. We have to become desperate enough for Him that nothing else matters in our lives but Him. Many people want to receive from God's hands, but they do not desire God. Many people expect the blessings and benefits that come from God, but they do not know Him, nor do they intend to get to know Him.

This part of the process is crucial as a building relies heavily upon a strong foundation. Matthew 6:33 reads, *"But seek ye first the Kingdom of God, and His righteousness; and all these things shall be added unto you."* God does not lie, and His Words are true. If we learn to love Him and put Him first in our lives, over our personal desires and above our problems, we will eventually find that those desires become a reality when we remain in His will.

I experienced this so many times. There were times I did not have to ask God for anything I desired outside of the spiritual, but I still received the things I desired dearly. I found then that Psalm 37:4, which says, *"Delight thyself also in the Lord: and He shall give thee the desires of thine heart,"* became a reality in my life.

As we seek God's face, His presence will begin to draw

near to us. The more we seek Him and the more we remain consistent, the more of Him or His presence we will find.

"Draw nigh to God, and He will draw nigh to you. Cleanse your hands, ye sinners; and purify your hearts, ye double-minded" (James 4:8).

As He reveals Himself to us, we will become more aware of our faults, attitudes, habits, and sins, and this is where the transforming work will begin within us, when we become aware of ourselves and the things that need to change.

A personal relationship with God is essential, especially if we desire His presence. If we need God's power to operate in and through our lives, it is even more critical for us not only to seek God for His presence but also to learn how to maintain His presence so that the evidence of His manifested presence noticeably remains with us. This type of relationship will be born only from obedience to God's Word, practicing love at all costs, and by living life in the Spirit, all of which intertwine.

"He that hath my commandments, and keepeth them, he it is that loveth me: and he that loveth me shall be loved of my Father, and I will love him, and will manifest myself to him. Judas saith unto him, not Iscariot, Lord, how is it that thou wilt manifest

> *thyself unto us, and not unto the world? Jesus answered and said unto him, If a man love me, he will keep my words: and my Father will love him, and we will come unto him, and make our abode with him"* (St. John 14:21-23).

The Holy Spirit showed me some time ago that we can only love by the Spirit of God, for God is love. God is also a Spirit, and they that worship Him must worship Him in spirit and in truth. Romans 8:8 says, *"Flesh cannot please God,"* and it is difficult, if possible at all, to love in the flesh; therefore, we can only love in the Spirit and by the Spirit of God, who enables us to do so.

If you want to know when you are constantly walking in the Spirit, check your love life. Do you love according to God's standards? Is your love life in alignment with the fruits of love according to 1 Corinthians 13? The truth of the matter is, sometimes we think we are walking in love, but we are far from expressing genuine love.

> *"But whoso hath this world's good, and seeth his brother have need, and shutteth up his bowels of compassion from him, how dwelleth the love of God in him? My little children, let us not love in word, neither in tongue; but in deed and in truth. And hereby we know that we are of the truth, and shall assure our hearts before him"* (1 John 3:17-19).

"But whoso keepeth his word, in him verily is the love of God perfected: hereby know we that we are in him. He that saith he abideth in him ought himself also so to walk, even as he walked" (1 John 2:5-6).

"Beloved, let us love one another: for love is of God; and every one that loveth is born of God, and knoweth God. He that loveth not knoweth not God; for God is love" (1 John 4:7-8).

This is what Smith Wigglesworth and Kathryn Cullman had (well-known Christian Evangelists). This is what the prophets of old had. This is what God has! Love! Abounding love, so much that He gave His life for you and me, to give us another chance to make things right so that we can live with Him in eternity; and we, too, need to have this Spirit of love.

If you are like me and you are 'sick and tired' of living a simple Christian life, if you desire to be far from ordinary, if your desire is for signs and wonders to follow you in the name of Jesus Christ, then this is our secret, to love as God loves, so that His presence can be manifested through us constantly. The presence of God brings an awareness of His love for us, and this love, once it abides within us, will be seen and felt by others. God's indwelling love will change and affect the lives of those we come in contact with as we become transporters of His presence, a medium through which God can operate to spread His love to others. This love is selfless, seeing the needs of others above its own.

Psalm 91 speaks more about His presence, keeping us from evil and overcoming the dragon. It reads:

> *"He that dwelleth in the secret place of the most high shall abide under the shadow of the Almighty. I will say of the Lord, He is my refuge and my fortress: my God; in him will I trust. Surely he shall deliver thee from the snare of the fowler, and from the noisome pestilence. He shall cover thee with his feathers, and under his wings shalt thou trust: his truth shall be thy shield and buckler. Thou shalt not be afraid for the terror by night; nor for the arrow that flieth by day; Nor for the pestilence that walketh in darkness; nor for the destruction that wasteth at noon day. A thousand shall fall at thy side and ten thousand at thy right hand; but it shall not come nigh thee. Only with thine eyes shalt thou behold and see the reward of the wicked. Because thou hast made the Lord, which is my refuge, even the most High, thy habitation; There shall no evil befall thee, neither shall any plague come nigh thy dwelling. For he shall give his angels charge over thee, to keep thee in all thy ways. They shall bear*

thee up in their hands, lest thou dash thy foot against a stone. Thou shalt tread upon the lion and adder: the young lion and the dragon shalt thou trample under feet. Because he hath set his love upon me, therefore will I deliver him: I will set him on high, because he hath known my name. He shall call upon me, and I will answer him: I will be with him in trouble; I will deliver him, and honour him. With long life will I satisfy him, and shew him my salvation."

The secret place of the Most-High is love, and to abide under the shadow of the Almighty means that we will always have God's presence with us, if we learn how to walk in love and live the love life. This is important. Verse seven says, *"A thousand shall fall at thy side, and ten thousand at thy right hand; but it shall not come nigh thee."* What a blessed promise. Did you get what verse ten said also? *"There shall no evil befall thee, 'NONE,' neither shall any plague come nigh thy dwelling because we have made love our habitation."* Sickness and diseases must flee, as these cannot live in the presence of God; they must die! The presence of God brings deliverance. God brings with Himself wholeness, completeness, healing, blessings, you name it. Nothing outside of these can stay in or on your body without God's permission once you get into His presence.

Being in God's presence means that we have resumed our rightful position in Christ, which is in the Spirit, and that elevates us to a higher position where we are seated together above in heavenly places with Christ (*Ephesians 2:6*).

Our position is above and not beneath. We are above our problems, above our struggles, above our situations, above the dragon, as verse thirteen of Psalm 91 says, and according to Luke 10:19, *"Above all* (we were given) *powers over the enemy."* This is how we get victory. By fighting from the correct position and by living our lives the right way, God has ordained—Life in the Spirit.

Notice what verse fifteen says: it did not say that trouble will not come. The presence of God may not keep us out of trouble, but what God promises us is deliverance in times of trouble.

> *"I will be glad and rejoice in thy mercy: for thou hast considered my trouble; thou hast known my soul in adversities; and hast not shut me up into the hand of the enemy: thou hast set my feet in a large room"* (Psalm 31:7-8).

God desires us to live a life without boundaries, limitations, borders, or walls in Him. It is time for the people of God to wake up and see what the devil is doing.

"Awake, awake, put on strength, O arm of the Lord; awake, as in the ancient days, in the generations of old. Art thou not it that hath cut Rahab, and wounded the dragon" (Isaiah 51:9)?

Isaiah 52:

¹"Awake, awake; put on thy strength, O Zion; put on thy beautiful garments, O Jerusalem, the holy city: for henceforth there shall no more come into thee the uncircumcised and the unclean.

²Shake thyself from the dust; arise and sit down, O Jerusalem: loose thyself from the bands of thy neck, O captive daughter of Zion.

³For thus saith the Lord, Ye have sold yourselves for nought; and ye shall be redeemed without money.

⁴For thus saith the Lord God, My people went down aforetime into Egypt to sojourn there; and the Assyrian oppressed them without cause.

⁵Now therefore, what have I here, saith the Lord, that my people is taken away for nought? Those who rule over them make them howl, saith the Lord; and my name is continually blasphemed every day.

⁶Therefore my people shall know my name: therefore they shall know in that day that I am he that doth speak: behold, it is I.

⁷How beautiful upon the mountains are the feet of him that bringeth good tidings, that publisheth peace; that bringeth good tidings of good, that publisheth salvation; that saith unto Zion, Thy God reigneth!

⁸Thy watchmen shall lift up the voice; with the voice together shall they sing: for they shall see eye to eye, when the Lord shall bring again Zion.

⁹Break forth into joy, sing together, ye waste places of Jerusalem: for the Lord hath comforted his people, he hath redeemed Jerusalem.

¹⁰The Lord hath made bare his holy arm in the eyes of all the nations; and all the ends of the earth shall see the salvation of our God.

¹¹Depart ye, depart ye, go ye out from thence, touch no unclean thing; go ye out of the midst of her; be ye clean, that bear the vessels of the Lord.

¹²*For ye shall not go out with haste, nor go by flight: for the Lord will go before you; and the God of Israel will be your reward.*

¹³*Behold, my servant shall deal prudently, he shall be exalted and extolled, and be very high.*

¹⁴*As many were astonied at thee; his visage was so marred more than any man, and his form more than the sons of men:*

¹⁵*So shall he sprinkle many nations; the kings shall shut their mouths at him: for that which had not been told them shall they see; and that which they had not heard shall they consider."*

Isaiah 35

¹*"The wilderness and the solitary place shall be glad for them; and the desert shall rejoice, and blossom as the rose.*

²*It shall blossom abundantly, and rejoice even with joy and singing: the glory of Lebanon shall be given unto it, the excellency of Carmel and Sharon, they shall see the glory of the Lord, and the excellency of our God.*

³Strengthen ye the weak hands, and confirm the feeble knees.

⁴Say to them that are of a fearful heart, Be strong, fear not: behold, your God will come with vengeance, even God with a recompense; he will come and save you.

⁵Then the eyes of the blind shall be opened, and the ears of the deaf shall be unstopped.

⁶Then shall the lame man leap as a hart, and the tongue of the dumb sing: for in the wilderness shall waters breakout, and streams in the desert.

⁷And the parched ground shall become a pool, and the thirsty land springs of water: in the habitation of dragons, where each lay, shall be grass with reeds and rushes.

⁸And a highway shall be there, and a way, and it shall be called the way of holiness; the unclean shall not pass over it; but it shall be for those: the wayfaring men, though fools, shall not err therein.

⁹No lion shall be there, nor any ravenous beast shall

go up there on, it shall not be found there; but the redeemed shall walk there:

[10] And the ransomed of the Lord shall return, and come to Zion with songs and everlasting joy upon their heads: they shall obtain joy and gladness, and sorrow and sighing shall flee away."

Reread verse nine of Isaiah 35. Praise Jesus! Every other beast associated with the dragon will have to flee!

We play a vital role in our deliverance. We have to get up and do what Isaiah 52 says, instead of sitting around doing nothing. Faith involves action, and even after we are delivered, it will take faith and living in God's presence to maintain our deliverance. Step out, and the Holy Spirit will direct and order those steps. Some battles are for the Lord to fight, but we are required to play our role in fighting battles by His leading. Remember the children of Israel? God delivered them and brought them out of Egypt. He fought for them, but when it was time for them to obtain the Promised Land–the territories God gave them, they had to get up and fight for it. It is high time the church woke up out of the sleep she is in and took back all that the enemy has stolen from her.

> "...the kingdom of heaven suffereth violence, and the violent take it by force" (Matthew 11:12).

The presence of God brings conviction, revelation, knowledge, healing, deliverance, victory over the powers of darkness, blessings, and so much more.

Remember the story of the Ark of God in 2 Samuel 6? When the Ark of God abode in the house of Obededom for three months, the Word of God declared the entire family was blessed. The ark of God represents God's presence. Where the presence of God is, there are blessings and fullness of joy.

"Beloved, I wish above all things that thou mayest prosper and be healthy, even as thy soul prospereth" (3 John 1:2).

It is God's desire for us to prosper and be in good health, but this can only be achieved if we refrain from sin and acquire His presence. The presence of God is key to victory in our lives; victory over the dragon, victory in every way. Once again, I implore you to seek the face of God, not His hands. Go after God with your entire heart, and the additions will eventually follow as you step out in faith, being led by God.

PRAYER POINTS

The Lord gave me two prayer points in a personal encounter with Him, and He showed me four other prayer points from the scriptures, so that I will be sharing six prayer points regarding the spirit of the dragon in this segment.

1. PLUCK ITS SCALES

I find this to be a significant point and the first to pray. The scales of the dragon act as a protective barrier. Before we can wound this or any other spirit, we first have to strip it of its power (read Matthew 12:29). The scales protect this spirit and others like it, and its confidence in not being harmed is built in its protective barrier (its scales).

Think about it. If something is covered with scales and you try to bore or penetrate it with a pointed instrument, depending on how hard or thick those scales are, it will never penetrate. Still, once the scales are removed, the delicate flesh beneath will be exposed and can be easily wounded.

Our words used in prayer act like a sword, and our lifestyle and faith in God fuel the effectiveness of our prayers (Hebrews 4:12, James 5:6).

2. BLIND OR PLUCK ITS EYES

As mentioned in earlier chapters, the dragon is known for its keen eyesight, and as a result of this, it can spot and devour your blessings even before you learn of them. Pluck its eyes or command blindness and confusion in Jesus' name.

3. BREAK ITS CLAWS and–

4. COMMAND IT TO VOMIT UP EVERYTHING IT HAS DEVOURED FOR YOU

If this spirit is going to capture you or anything with your name written on it, it is going to be either in its grip, in its belly, or in both places. Many times, our happiness, our health, our prosperity/finance, our marriage, our jobs, opportunities, etc., are held captive in the claws of this beast or in its belly. Take authority and command a supernatural release to every area of your life bound by this spirit in Jesus' name.

5. SLAY ITS NECK

After warfare between you and this spirit, it would make no sense to wound it, take back what is rightfully yours, and leave it. It would only regain strength to return and do more harm, so slay it or command it to die in Jesus' name.

6. BREAK THE POWERS OF DARKNESS & EVERY EVIL ATTACHMENT FROM OVER YOUR LIFE

Keep in mind that the devil has an entire army for himself, so constant prayer and warfare are needed. As you overcome one spirit, another will try to invade your life, so complete deliverance lies solely in remaining in the presence of God. Just remember that this is a constant war between good and evil, God and the devil, his demons and us. We must have made up our minds to fight until Jesus comes back for us, His children. After all, there is a reason why we are referred to as 'soldiers' in the Bible. We must fight to the end without backing out or giving up. We are not alone. We have God's angels who fight on our behalf. Fight with one aim in mind, and that is to overcome by enduring to the end.

"Fight the good fight of faith, lay hold on eternal life..." (1 Timothy 6:12).

"I have fought a good fight, I have finished my course, I have kept the faith." (2 Timothy 4:7).

So, the *ATTACK STRATEGY* I used after studying and learning about my opponent was: to disarm and weaken, then launch an attack, take back what is mine by faith, destroy the powers of darkness, and walk away in victory. From this point forward, thank God for victory, seal your blessings, be alert, and remain watchful.

TIP

There is an unseen war taking place in the spiritual realm, and it is our responsibility to fight for what God has given us by praying and walking in obedience to God.

Do you remember the story of Daniel? Daniel prayed to God, and his prayer was answered from the first day he prayed, but the answer was delayed because of the unseen war taking place between angels and principalities in the air.

When we pray, angels are assigned to fight on our behalf and to establish God's will in our lives here on earth. Our prayers play a significant role in warfare, as angels will partner with us to fight on our behalf.

The Lord told me to pray these prayer points at night because it is at night that this spirit gains strength. Many of us already know that 12:00 am–3:00 am is referred to as the hour of evil. These are the hours when demonic activity is most prevalent. The devil loves darkness, and nighttime is his time to do all sorts of evil when we are asleep.

Many Christians fall short in this area: we may make time to pray during the day, but little or no prayer is done at night due to sleep, which gives the devil an edge over us. Prayerlessness or ceasing to pray gives the devil's agents time to regain strength. This is one reason the Bible says, *"Men ought always to pray and not to faint,"* and also to

"Pray without ceasing." This can be accomplished by living in the Spirit.

The beautiful thing about all of this, however, is that once we live our lives in the Spirit, the Holy Spirit will grant us a level of awareness and alert us to danger whenever trouble approaches, even in our sleep. The Holy Spirit is watching, and God's angels will alert us and fight for us in times of trouble. God will never leave us; He will always be with us even to the end of this world; Amen.

5
A WORD OF CAUTION

I was amazed at the immediate results I started to achieve while praying these prayer points. I began to receive great ideas from the Holy Spirit; ideas that worked. My health improved quickly, our finances stabilized, and the list goes on.

Let me add, I was told I needed to do two surgeries, and today, without the performance of any surgical procedure or medical intervention, I am healed by the power of God.

During my encounter, God told me that I was healed, and it was during that time that I learned what was causing me severe pain to the point where walking became extremely difficult. I was told that I had a massive kidney stone that needed to be removed surgically by breaking it into small pieces. By then, I was bedridden as pain injections no longer worked, but God told me that I was healed before I received the results from the tests that I did, so I was stunned to hear the doctor's report.

I know that God is real and His Words mean so much more to me than the reports of doctors, so I decided to claim my healing by getting up out of bed in faith. With tears in my eyes from the excruciating pain I felt, I became violent and stood on the Word of God, taking back my health by force. This went on for about two weeks, and then it happened.

One morning, while lying in bed after waking, I felt intense pressure on my back, as though someone were standing on it. I tried to find a comfortable position, but the pressure persisted for about 20 minutes, no matter what position I wriggled into. After that intense pressure lifted, it was replaced by intense heat in that same area for another twenty minutes or so. At that point, I realized that something supernatural was happening. God was honouring His Word and my faith. He had brought my healing to me, and there in my bedroom, my kidney was healed. Since that experience, I have been totally healed and pain-free from kidney stones, praise God. My healing did not come easily; I had to get radical and fight for it, but God honoured His Word and my faith, praise God.

There was another condition that I got healed of sometime later, but this healing did not come miraculously. Doctors were unable to diagnose me, but the Holy Spirit drew my attention to my passionate craving for sweet treats. The Holy Spirit prompted me to begin monitoring my sugar intake as I became aware that my condition was due to the hormone insulin. Within a few weeks, I started to see improvements. Whenever I consumed excess sugar, the condition exaggerated, and whenever I withdrew or cut back on my sugar intake, the symptoms subsided. I understood immediately what God required of me. It was time for me to grow up and be disciplined, because I was not about to have everything handed to me easily. My healing was in my hands; it was my responsibility to take control of my sugar cravings to be healed, and this is what I did.

Some healing will be miraculous, some through medicines or other medical interventions, and others through changing or monitoring what we eat or how we eat. Our psychological aspect plays a vital role in health, so it should be considered as well.

Everything fell into perspective. I stopped my pressure medication, and the pressure readings that seemed impossible to heal at first returned to normal without the use of drugs.

We were now able to live a better life. The life we dreamed of could now be seen as an obvious possibility. Things got really great, and most importantly, my relationship with God excelled. I had a better understanding of my purpose, the Ministry to which God has called me, and my desires were now becoming a reality.

I was thrilled, enthused, excited, and encouraged by the transformation. I was free; I was liberated for the first time in my life.

I have discovered that before true happiness can be established, your purpose and destiny must first be realized. Your happiness is tied to your destiny. Happiness outside of purpose will vanish, but happiness that is discovered through an identity with Christ will last for a lifetime.

People need to identify the purpose for which they were created. Besides worshiping God, each person here on earth has a unique mission to accomplish (this, too, is a form of worship).

Once you discover this God-given mission, you will be sure of it, as something within you will resonate, a desire will be born, and joy will ignite. Understanding your purpose is essential.

I knew without a doubt that something was broken. The curse had been lifted, and we were set free. I felt as free as a bird and as light as a feather, and the transformation affected every area of my life, so much so that it became apparent to others.

I found this interesting because even people who were not familiar with me became attracted to me. People wanted to know who I was and what I did, and they began to request marital advice and lifestyle counseling. No one had to ask if I was a Child of God. I constantly received comments in this area about how my relationship with God was blooming and that His presence was with me.

It was at this point that I realized that I had really been living in bondage. Everything became clear regarding why my husband and I were having so many struggles in our relationship and in moving forward in every way. God had finally spoken. He had finally revealed the hindrance in our lives, and this spirit is hindering a lot of people today, but the curse can be broken, praise God.

This did not come easily. This revelation came only out of an intense, heartfelt search for God. It came out of a hunger for Him; it came out of desperation for Him. This came out of a pulling and a tugging that the Holy Spirit did as He saw me seeking after Him.

As I drew closer to God, all I wanted was more of Him. I wanted nothing of the devil and nothing from the devil to be seen or left in me. This included worry, doubt, fear, anxiety, anger, you name it. I realized I was bound to an extent and needed deliverance, and this desperate drive to be free from all evil and its effects, and to be Holy just as Christ is, drove me to an intense search where I would be purged and brought into the presence of God. This was just the beginning, and I discovered God in a way I never expected. It can be you, too.

As I've said before, praying these prayer points alone will not be enough. Your lifestyle is essential, and your priorities must be right. *Do not pray for financial wealth or* riches. *Do not pray for the benefits; instead, cultivate a genuine desire to meet the one who gives all the benefits, to know Him more.* It has to come from a genuine love for God, where you desire to please Him so much because of who He is, and then the benefits will automatically follow. Fall in love with Jesus and get your priorities and motives right.

The Holy Spirit will begin to lead you in the paths and avenues He wants you to venture. He will tell you how to pray, when to pray, and what to pray for, and the revelations unique to your situation will begin to flow. Our duty is to live a life pleasing before God and to pray continually as God gives utterance. God is the one who gives directions and instructions, reveals knowledge, pours out, and adds to our lives. *Our job is never to seek after additions or overflow, but to wait on the Lord to direct us and grant us our blessings in His time; and in due season,* He will. Oh, if we learn to wait on God, things would become so much better for us.

Do you remember the disciple, Peter? Peter walked with Jesus, talked with Him, prayed with Him, and watched Him perform numerous miracles, but still Peter did not know Him; he was not converted. Jesus knew this, and that is why He said to him, *"Peter, when thou art converted, strengthen ye the brethren."* Peter's conversion did not take place until the day of Pentecost when the Holy Spirit descended upon each person gathered in the upper room, and they were all filled with the Holy Ghost. Peter preached that day, and 3,000 people were saved. He was fearful before his conversion, so much so that he denied Christ, but after his transformation, he was endued with power and boldness from on high that he became willing to die a similar death to Jesus. Peter was changed, totally transformed. When you are converted, you will know it. Your desires will change, your priorities will change, your appetite will change, your goals will change, and you will change. The church is in a mess. People are caught up in wealth and material things; their hearts are not centered on God, and the only way out of this is to be converted.

There is a process everyone must go through before receiving what God has for them, and there is no escaping it. People are getting so accustomed to a microwave mentality or a 'get wealthy quickly' mindset, and this is already in the church. As soon as prayers are prayed, people are unwilling to wait on God for an answer if it tarries; they want it now. As a result, they go outside God's will to achieve things, and in most instances, anyone who does that will end up back at square one, right where they started, if they humble themselves and return to God. God will strip you to teach you humility, patience, and obedience.

The sooner we humble ourselves and allow God to have His way in our lives, the sooner we will get what He has for us. God is in no hurry, and if we are not careful, we will find ourselves in the same spot or position for a long time. Remember the children of Israel when God delivered them out of Egypt? What could have taken them 11 days took them 430 years! Did you get that comparison? It took them *YEARS, compared* to *DAYS!* Oh, how sad. Some of them died without inheriting the promises, and this will be *YOU* if you refuse to submit yourself entirely to God and go through your process by allowing Him to lead you, instead of trying to lead God. God does not work that way. All He requires from you is your obedience in doing *YOUR* part. Are you having a wilderness experience right now?

If we really want God to be involved in our lives, we must learn to get ourselves out of the way. If we genuinely want to see God move in our lives, we must learn how to trust Him. We must learn how to put our flesh under subjection by the Spirit of God. God's Spirit needs to be in control of our lives, but He can't be until we allow Him. We must remain sensitive and continually examine ourselves to see if we are in God's way, preventing Him from working freely on our behalf.

Sensitivity is crucial. It takes the wisdom of God to fight and to overcome. This remains true when fighting against the spirit of the dragon. I have learnt by experience that this is a very stubborn and rebellious demon that will fight for you at all costs. I have discovered that when you believe you are free from this spirit, it will return to try and regain control of your life. You must remain constant and persistent in your lifestyle and prayer life.

So, things were going great for my family. My husband and I became one for the first time after seven years of marriage, and our fantasies were no longer just fantasies but a reality. I always believed in God for a good life, but to be truthful, I didn't expect it to begin so soon. Shortly after enjoying the blessings that God was giving us, we began to experience a little struggle here and there again. It baffled me, so I started reflecting and spoke with my husband, as his concerns were also expressed. It was at that point that I recall becoming tired and easing off a bit from nighttime prayer. Could this be the result of not praying these points at night? I resumed nighttime prayer, and within days, we experienced a turnaround once again. The same thing happened again: I got exhausted and fell asleep, and the moment I resumed praying the points, we experienced an almost sudden change. Was God making a statement? Was God showing me that the lifestyle alone was not enough, but that both lifestyle and prayer were?

In reality, not praying the prayer points given meant I was disobedient, as God instructed me to pray them. Failure to do so meant I was in violation of God's commands, and disobedience leads to sin. I struggled to correct this, but each night I tried to take back my stand, this spirit would literally overpower me with deep sleep. I knew this was not normal; the dragon was putting up a fight.

I have come to realize that if you are not adamant and determined when fighting this spirit, it will regain control of your life, your situation, your blessings, and you. We need to have a made-up mind, willing to fight to the end for what is rightfully ours.

This spirit is intimidating and will use fear to oppose you, turning people against you. Your entire life could turn upside down in an instant when warring against this spirit, but God will not allow evil to overcome good. Pause now and re-read Job 41, which talks about the spirit of Leviathan. The dragon spirit has the potential to make people fearful of opposing it.

Here are a few verses from Job 41 again that will highlight the power and potential of this spirit. It is not afraid to fight back, and to overcome, you must remain steadfast in prayer and in the presence of God.

> *[10] None is so fierce that dare stir him up: who then is able to stand before me?*
>
> *[11] Who hath prevented me, that I should repay him? Whatsoever is under the whole heaven is mine.*
>
> *[22] In his neck remaineth strength, and sorrow is turned into joy before him.*

^{24} His heart is as firm as a stone; yea, as hard as a piece of the nether millstone.

^{25} When he raiseth up himself, the mighty are afraid: by reason of breakings they purify themselves.

^{26} The sword of him that layeth at him cannot hold: the spear, the dart, nor the habergeon.

^{27} He esteemeth iron as straw, and brass as rotten wood.

^{28} The arrow cannot make him flee: slingstones are turned with him into stubble.

^{29} Darts are counted as stubble: he laugheth at the shaking of a spear.

^{33} Upon earth there is not his like, who is made without fear.

Once you are in right standing with God and you pray these prayer points, you will see the effects. God is not partial; He is a just God, and I pray and know that what He did for us, He will do for you. Do not be fearful; be willing to resist this spirit, fight for what is yours, and you will overcome with God's help.

Believe it and do not fall into the deception that this is just a myth or a fairytale. This has been a reality in my family's life, and I have never had prayers answered this quickly when praying from a place of obedience. It is very easy to fall back into old habits, so be careful that this spirit does not trick you into believing you are not delivered when you really are. Being alert is key to maintaining your deliverance. *Do not fall back into old habits; beware!*

Revelation 12 gives a good picture of this spirit at work and how God will fight for us.

> *[1] "And there appeared a great wonder in heaven; a woman clothed with the sun, and the moon under her feet, and upon her head a crown of twelve stars:*
>
> *[2] And she being with child cried, travailing in birth, and pained to be delivered.*
>
> *[3] And there appeared another wonder in heaven; and behold a great red dragon, having seven heads and ten horns, and seven crowns upon his heads.*
>
> *[4] And his tail drew the third part of the stars of heaven, and did cast them to the earth: and the dragon stood before the woman which was ready to be delivered, for to devour her child as soon as it was born.*

⁵And she brought forth a man child, who was to rule all nations with a rod of iron: and her child was caught up unto God, and to his throne.

⁶And the woman fled into the wilderness, where she hath a place prepared of God that they should feed her there a thousand two hundred and three score days.

⁷And there was war in heaven: Michael and his angels fought against the dragon; and the dragon fought and his angels,

⁸And prevailed not; neither was their place found any more in heaven.

⁹And the great dragon was cast out, that old serpent, called the Devil, and Satan, which deceiveth the whole world: he was cast out into the earth, and his angels were cast out with him.

¹⁰And I heard a loud voice saying in heaven, now is come salvation, and strength, and the kingdom of our God, and the power of his Christ: for the accuser of our brethren is cast down, which accused them before our God day and night.

¹¹And they overcame him by the blood of the Lamb, and by the word of their testimony; and they loved not their lives unto the death.

¹²Therefore rejoice, ye heavens, and ye that dwell in them. Woe to the inhabiters of the earth and of the sea! For the devil is come down unto you, having great wrath, because he knoweth that he hath but a short time.

¹³And when the dragon saw that he was cast unto the earth, he persecuted the woman which brought forth the man child.

¹⁴And to the woman were given two wings of a great eagle, that she might fly into the wilderness, into her place, where she is nourished for a time, and times, and half a time, from the face of the serpent.

¹⁵And the serpent cast out of his mouth water as a flood after the woman, that he might cause her to be carried away of the flood.

¹⁶And the earth helped the woman, and the earth opened her mouth, and swallowed up the flood which the dragon cast out of his mouth.

A WORD OF CAUTION

> *^{17}And the dragon was wroth with the woman, and went to make war with the remnant of her seed, which keep the commandments of God, and have the testimony of Jesus Christ."*

Believers, the war is on. The battle is hot and getting hotter, but God has given us a tool to use in warring against the powers of darkness. This is it! It has worked for my family and me, and it's yours to use too. Will you believe?

Did you know that the Earth's elements can either fight for us or against us? In witchcraft, witches and satanist use these as aids in their spiritual fight against people, but they are 'copy cats' of God's original design.

A true Believer cannot be affected by such if we remain in the presence of God. The earth, the wind, water, fire, and all the elements combined will not cooperate with our enemies if we truly live for Christ, but instead, will fight against our enemies on our behalf. Just re-read the above passage once again (Revelation 12).

It pays to serve God sincerely!

6
SAMPLE PRAYER

Father, in the name of Jesus Christ of Nazareth, I stand now in faith as your daughter. I arise to my rightful position, which is in heavenly places according to Ephesians chapter two. I ask that as I take my stand, you will increase, and I decrease. May you be seen and heard in me above all else. Strip me from self, oh God. Cause my spirit to be naked before your eyes. Blot out my transgressions and remove sin from between us. Clothe me in your righteousness and with the armour of God. Prepare me now, fit for your presence and equipped for war.

I come against the spirit of the dragon in Jesus' name. I pluck its scales, and I blind its eyes. I strip it of its power, and I prophecy and declare that this spirit will no longer be able to spot or steal my blessings anymore. I enter now into the camp of the enemy to take back that which is rightfully mine.

I break the claws of the dragon, and I command everything within its grip to be released now! Release (call out areas of your life under attack), my marriage, release my finances, release my health, and my family in the name of Jesus! Release my peace, release my joy, release my happiness in Jesus' name.

I hold you, spirit of the dragon, by the neck, and I command you to cough, spew, or vomit everything that you have consumed for me in Jesus' name! Vomit up the opportunities, vomit up the innovative ideas, vomit up the car, the house, the pregnancy. Vomit up all my substance and blessings that you have stolen from me in Jesus' name!

I command you to fall from your throne! Fall from the heavenlies! I dethrone you now, and I declare that as you fall, you will never be able to rise again in the precious name of our Lord.

I slay your neck, I crush your head, and I speak death to you in Jesus' name. I command you to die in the name of Jesus. I break your powers over my life forever, and I declare that I am loosed and set free by the power of the Holy Ghost.

I declare that everything you have stripped me of will be restored double in Jesus' name. I speak death to you now, and I declare that everything which has my name on it will be supernaturally marked by the power of God and never be devoured again in the name of Jesus.

I cut off every evil cycle from my life; it stops here! I

sever every evil connection to my body, soul, and spirit in the name of Jesus. I pray that the scales will be removed from my eyes and the veil broken from off my mind. I declare that you have no more power over my family or me forever in the name of Jesus.

I pray Father that you will increase my knowledge and sharpen my spiritual eyesight to see the devil from afar before he launches his attack. I come against every satanic swallowing and every satanic backlash in Jesus' name.

I thank you for freeing me now from the powers of the enemy. I thank you that every evil work done against my life is destroyed. Thank you for restoration, and I thank you in advance for your divine protection from the powers of darkness, here on and forever more; Amen!

> *Although other creatures are associated with the dragon, your primary focus should be to attack the dragon spirit in prayer unless the Holy Spirit instructs you otherwise. This method will eradicate all creatures associated. I questioned the Lord about this, and this is what He said to me: "If you wake up every morning and remove cobwebs visible, you are going to have to be prepared to do this often, as the spider will always be making more cobwebs once it's around. You will be giving yourself more work. If you want to get rid of the cobweb, get rid of the spider." That analogy erased my concerns.*

If you want to get rid of the underlying spirits that carry out evil assignments on behalf of the king spirits, get rid of the head spirit. I understand perfectly why He gave me the Revelation of the dragon. Get rid of the dragon, and you will conquer other spirits associated with the dragon and your problems.

He then said to me, "Anything I do is well done," and I'll end on that note. You don't need to add any prayer points about the dragon spirit, and you do not need to frustrate yourself praying the same points for all other creatures involved unless the Holy Spirit leads you to. God knows what He is doing, and anything He does is well done.

Instead of focusing on the obvious spirits at work in your life and binding these spirits individually, such as the spirit of poverty, anger, fear, infirmity, and so on, ask the Lord to reveal the king spirit behind your struggles and attack that spirit in prayer. Once that spirit is defeated, you will conquer your problems.

MORE PRAYER POINTS

I find that praying back the Word of God is a powerful

SAMPLE PRAYER

way to pray when your life aligns with God's Word. There are tons of prayer points we can use from the scriptures for various situations, but I've selected a few of my favorites to share in this chapter.

They are as follows:

1) Break the staff of the wicked and the scepter of the rulers – (Isaiah 14:5)
2) No weapon formed against me shall prosper, and every tongue that rises up against me in judgment I will condemn. I condemn now the mouths of my enemies. I condemn the mouths of those who plot evil against me and seek my hurt. I condemn the mouths of witches, satanists, and warlocks operating against my life in Jesus' name – (Isaiah 54:17)
3) Shut the mouth of the lions – (Daniel 6:22)
4) Arise now in my life, oh God, and let my enemies be scattered–(Psalm 68:1)
5) Loose the bands of wickedness – (Isaiah 58:6)
6) Undo the heavy burdens – (Isaiah 58:6)
7) Let the oppressed go free – (Isaiah 58:6)
8) Break every yoke – (Isaiah 58:6)
9) I take now the keys you have given me, and I bind__ and I loose__ in Jesus' name – (Matthew 16:19)
10) Upon this rock I will build my church, and the gates of hell shall not prevail against it – (Matthew 16:18)

11) Clothe me in your Spirit; let your Spirit rest upon me – (Isaiah 11:2)

12) I bind the spirit of error, and I release the Spirit of truth in my life – (1 John 4:6)

13) There are the workers of iniquity fallen, they are cast down and shall not be able to rise – (Psalm 36:12)

14) I fly every trap that is set for me – (Psalm 31:4)

15) Cause them that are against me to be put to shame and brought to confusion – (Psalm 35:4)

16) Create in me a clean heart and renew a right Spirit within me – (Psalm 51:10)

17) Let nothing of the devil be found within me, oh God – (1 John 3:8, 9)

18) Let nothing separate my spirit from yours; blot out all my sins – (Psalm 66:18; 51:9)

19) Plead my cause, oh Lord, fight against them that fight against me – (Psalm 35:1)

20) Let justice and truth prevail in our lives – (Isaiah 59:4)

21) Let your judgment be executed now – (Isaiah 61:8)

22) Grant unto me your wisdom in all its fullness – (James 1:5)

23) As it is in heaven, so let it be here on earth. Let your will be done and thine only – (Matthew 6:10)

24) The battle is the Lord's – (1 Samuel 17:47)

25) God has not given me a spirit of fear, but of love, power, and of a sound mind – (2 Timothy 1:7)

26) We are more than conquerors – (Romans 8:37)

27) Save my enemies and cause them to see themselves, but if they desire my hurt and refuse to turn, destroy them that are against me with double destruction – (Jeremiah 17:18)
28) Revenge me of my persecutors – (Jeremiah 15:15)
29) Pour the Spirit of grace and supplication upon us – (Zechariah 12:10)

As mentioned in the introduction to this book, I have come to understand the insertion of Psalm 23 (in the shared dream). Psalm 23 is a reflection of Psalm 91 coming to pass in our lives. If we truly understand Psalm 91, we will realize there is no need to fear, as Psalm 23 offers insight into the mighty deliverance that will follow. I love how the Psalmist David puts it:

> *"The Lord is my shepherd; I shall not want. He maketh me to lie down in green pastures: he leadeth me beside the still waters. He restoreth my soul: he leadeth me in the paths of righteousness for his name's sake. Yea, though I walk through the valley of the shadow of death, I will fear no evil: for thou art with me; thy rod and thy staff they comfort me. Thou preparest a table before me in the presence of mine enemies: thou anointest my head with oil; my cup runneth over. Surely goodness and mercy shall follow me all the days of*

> *my life: and I will dwell in the house of the Lord forever."*

What power! It pays to know God and to have a blessed hope and assurance in Him, praise Jesus.

When we come to that place in God where our lifestyle is born of holiness, God is forced to fight on our behalf. When we live for God, God will fight for us. Holiness attracts the presence of God, and His presence will protect and keep us.

Without righteousness, God will not hear or answer our prayers. A righteous lifestyle requires action and obedience to prove our commitment to God. We need to get practical and come to that place in God where His presence overshadows and protects us. We need to reach a place where our enemies must first go through God before reaching us. It should be every Believer's aim to live a life of holiness that will keep us in the presence of God.

God's presence is everything. It will overshadow us so that we can always be victorious even when we are asleep. What a blessed life. We have already overcome!

EPILOGUE

I solemnly declare that the information given in this book is tried and true. This is not a figment of my imagination but a revelation given to me by God for the problems I personally faced. Within a short time frame after seeking God and receiving this revelation about the spirit of the dragon, I began to see results, and things have never been the same in my life. My husband is a living testament to this, as one of the most outstanding results for us has been in our finances.

I am confident that this revelation holds not only the key to victory in warfare, but also to our lives. Once you decide to walk pure before God by choosing to put off sin (*shun the very appearance of evil*) and embrace righteousness, seek God for who He is, pray these points, and victory will be yours also by the power of the Holy Spirit.

After all is said and done, I encourage you to seek God for yourself concerning your personal situation, as there is so much more to be revealed. Do not pray with anxious expectations, but pray, believing and trusting God to do what He will in His timing.

God is not a genie we can rub or manipulate to get the things we desire when we want them. God is in control of our lives, and He knows what's best for us. Our responsibility is to seek God, do what is required, live a Holy life, be patient, and remain faithful in prayer, knowing that things are working out behind the scenes for our good, even when it may not look like it. Things will fall into place eventually when we least expect them.

I prayed to God for years, on and off, asking Him about my situation, but it was not until I truly surrendered and began to walk pure before Him that He revealed the spirit of the dragon at work in my life. This revelation came out of an intense search, a deep-rooted desperation to hear from God, and this was what moved Him, along with purity. I became a committed doer of the Word and not just a hearer.

I guarantee that if you get desperate enough for God to speak about your situation, He will. If you get quiet before Him, you will hear Him when He speaks, because God is always talking to us, but sometimes we become too busy to settle down and listen.

If you are hungry enough for God, you will search with

your entire heart and not stop until you find Him and become filled. Are you willing to get desperate for Him? Are you willing to lead a pure life according to God's standards? Sin separates us from God and blocks the flow of God's blessings in our lives. How desperate are you?

DEAR READERS

I have known Terryann Scott all her life and have lived with both her and her husband for thirteen years. I have witnessed their struggles not just financially, but otherwise, including the death of their first child, Danaevia Ashley Scott.

Throughout their pain and suffering, they have learned to remain faithful to God while holding onto their integrity. Throughout their disappointments, they drew closer to God, encouraging others likewise to fight on and to hope in God.

I know what they have been through, and watching them and their faith in action has encouraged me and deepened my faith. Psalm 91 and praying the points in attacking the spirit of the dragon have not only worked for them, but I, too, can testify that areas of my life that were blocked have been transformed.

To God be all the glory, and may He continue to prosper them.

Rev. Aneita Brown
Senior Pastor
Living Waters Christian Center (LWCC) Mandeville, Jamaica

> *Reverend Brown is a walking miracle, bearing the testimony of being raised from the dead in June of 2011. The Reverend died in Atlanta, Georgia, while on vacation visiting her son and family, but God brought her back from the dead to life, not once, but twice! Her story is documented in the book "Coming Back from the Dead: A True Story," available on Amazon and other retail sites.*

ABOUT THE AUTHOR

Change your thoughts, change your world; transform your future. Your mind is powerful. It can affect lives through a recognized, established pattern of thinking, and Terryann is on a mission to transform lives by transforming minds through the Word of God.

Minister Scott is the author of the powerful, life-changing series entitled "No More," among other works. Her writings are steered towards spiritual warfare, personal development, inner healing, and spiritual upliftment, providing *"Empowerment for the Total You."*

Her writings have impacted many and are tried, true, and inspired by the Holy Spirit. Mrs. Scott is also an Educator, Speaker, Publisher, and Workshop Facilitator, among other things. She carries the mandate of helping married couples and also those who are abused and broken. Her ministry seeks to help persons to "identify their purpose and walk into their God-given destiny." She is passionate about spreading the undiluted Gospel across the globe, and watching the power of God return in the church to restore broken lives through Healing and Deliverance is just a part of her vision.

Minister Scott believes knowledge is power, and, in alignment with this, her mission is to educate, motivate, encourage, and foster growth through workshops and other coaching sessions.

Terryann's voice is instituted to nurture and restore the body of Christ by revealing hidden truths while exploring matters of the heart that will enable the end-time army of God to regain her actual shape and form in Christ. She is very passionate about transforming lives and fulfilling her call according to Isaiah 61: 1-4; which is to "Heal the brokenhearted, set the oppressed free, comfort those who mourn, and to deliver those who are bound by the proclamation of the Gospel of Jesus Christ, in Spirit and power through the working of the Holy Spirit." Her messages can be heard internationally on the airwaves in some parts of the USA and the Caribbean.

Minister Scott has appeared in several magazines and has contributed to two published works in addition to her own.

Terryann is married to Praise and Worship Leader, Danever Scott, who is also a Minister of Religion, Producer, and Sound Engineer, among other things. The couple has three beautiful children together – Danaevia, Judah, and Kayla Scott, of whom the first is deceased. Through much heartache and pain, the couple has attained a closer walk with God, and they continue to share their story, offering hope to many.

LET'S CONNECT

Do you have a Supernatural Encounter you would like to share? Submit your stories to *info.scottspublishing@gmail.com* along with your full name, location, and occupation. Submissions will be collated and published as an eBook. Your experience matters and may be what someone needs to hear.

Connect with me on Facebook (don't forget to like my page) and on other social media sites such as X, YouTube, and Instagram.

May God bless you, and I do look forward to connecting.

LET'S CONNECT

For updates and new releases, follow me on Amazon.

Please submit a review for this devotional HERE. Your reviews are essential and will help others to find this free devotional guide. Your reviews will also help spread the message of the Gospel and inner healing to others across the globe. Tell your family and friends about this free devotional and invite them to download it. This guide may be precisely what they need during difficult times.

* * *

Check out my other titles.

BOOKS BY TERRYANN SCOTT

------

*To see a complete list on Amazon, please click **here***

The Revelation of the Dragon: No More Walls - Vol. 1 of "The 'No More' Series"

MY ENTIRE LIFE CHANGED, AND YOURS

CAN TOO by simply utilizing this powerful warfare strategy that God has released for His people.

"The Revelation of the Dragon: No More Walls" exposes the forces of darkness behind the longstanding cycles of disappointment, setbacks, fear, confusion, lack, poverty, and so much more.

This revelation came at the most trying and difficult time of my life, and it led me on a journey of self-discovery and a search for God. After my husband and I radically sought God, God stepped in, delivered our family, and revealed the culprit that was behind our struggles. I recognized almost immediately that a terribly longstanding cycle of pain, misery, and carry-overs was broken from our lives with very little effort on our part, except by being obedient to God and through maintaining a closer walk with Him.

BOOKS BY TERRYANN SCOTT

Roads to Success: No More Barriers - Vol. 2 of *"The 'No More' Series"*

Every person has a strong man governing their life, and to be successful, that strong man must first be identified and defeated. In Volume 1, *The Revelation of the Dragon: No More Walls*, Terryann Scott exposes a powerful spirit behind long-standing struggles such as disappointments, dryness, and lack in people's lives.

In Volume 2, *Roads to Success: No More Barriers*, Minister Scott reveals two hidden paths and five main roads you'll want to travel on for guaranteed success.

Mrs. Scott unfolds the heart of God towards His people while exposing seven Biblical Processes and four Biblical Principles that will transform your life from barrenness to fruitfulness.

In this book, you will:

- Learn the seven Biblical Processes and four Biblical Principles for guaranteed success.
- Discover how your past may be holding you back.
- Identify hidden blocks from your past and learn how to overcome them.
- Discover the heart of God, His promises towards His children, and how to acquire them.
- Discover the role of your obedience to God.
- Identify 'roads' to travel on daily for guaranteed success and
- Learn how you can use the law of attraction by God's design to create the life you've always dreamed of, God's way.

Do not stop here, a new life awaits you! I know you will be blessed.

"Your success in life is not determined by God, but by your obedience to Him."
~ Terryann Scott.

BOOKS BY TERRYANN SCOTT

Keys to the Kingdom: Unlocking the Mysteries of Prayer

Why are some prayers answered and not others? Why does a good God allow bad things to happen to people? Why am I praying, but I'm not getting my prayers answered? Is God real? If you are curious about the Mysteries of the Kingdom and how to get your prayers answered, then this book is for you.

In this book, Minister Terryann Scott shares personal stories and testimonies from spiritual encounters with Jesus and supernatural revelations received in the spiritual realm.

Just as there are laws that govern the formation of water into ice, so too there are spiritual laws that govern prayer. If these laws are not understood and if the conditions required for prayer are not met, our prayers will not be answered.

BOOKS BY TERRYANN SCOTT

I am so excited to share with you what the Lord has taught me about prayer and Kingdom power. Join me now for this intense read as we take a peek into the supernatural realm to discover how to get your prayers answered and unlock the Mystery of Prayer.

BOOKS BY TERRYANN SCOTT

Becoming a Better You: Heal Your Soul; Heal Your Life

Unhealthy patterns and cycles are the result of a wounded soul that needs to be healed. Life's challenges can leave us beaten and worn, and the anxiety, worry, stress, and other adverse effects associated with the struggles we endure can prevent us from shining like the person we were created to be. A toxic mind will lead to a toxic life, and if you desire a healthy life, you have to acquire a healthy mind and a free spirit. Discover how to get healed from the soul level and give birth to your God-given destiny by using this three-step strategy that God has given me.

A new life awaits you. It's time to become a better you! Let's go!

BOOKS BY TERRYANN SCOTT

Surviving Challenging Times: Faith Devotional

Why does God allow hardship? Where is He when life feels overwhelming? Does He truly care?

These are the questions many believers wrestle with during seasons of pain, loss, uncertainty, and waiting. When challenges arise, it can be difficult to think clearly or hold onto hope—especially when fear, anxiety, and discouragement begin to take root.

Surviving Challenging Times was created for those moments.

This 21-week devotional is designed to strengthen your faith, renew your mind, and uplift your spirit when life feels heavy. Through weekly reflections grounded in Scripture and faith-filled encouragement, this devotional gently guides you to see beyond your circumstances and rediscover God's presence, love, and purpose—even in the midst of difficulty.

Rather than merely helping you endure, *Surviving Challenging Times* challenges you to grow. It inspires a new way of thinking rooted in trust, hope, and spiritual resilience, so you can move from merely surviving to experiencing the blessings of steadfast faith.

If you are feeling drained, burdened, discouraged, or uncertain about the future, this devotional will help you refocus your heart on God's truth and promises.

Are you ready to strengthen your faith and rise above life's challenges?

Join this 21-week journey of reflection, renewal, and spiritual growth—and discover how faith can carry you through even the most challenging seasons.

BOOKS BY TERRYANN SCOTT

Overcoming Obstacles: Hope Devotional
eBook available FREE on popular retailer sites

Are you struggling with inner fears, emotional wounds, or the desire to give up?

Forgiving those who have caused deep pain—and finding the confidence to move forward after broken relationships—can feel overwhelming. Lingering memories, damaged self-worth, and unhealed emotions often keep us stuck. Yet healing is possible with guidance, faith, and a renewed way of thinking.

Overcoming Obstacles is an inner-healing devotional guide designed to help you heal your heart, renew your mind, and rediscover your God-given purpose. Every person was designed with intention, but before purpose can be fully revealed and fulfilled, the heart must be restored, and the mind transformed.

This devotional is written for those facing emotional

and mental challenges, especially believers who struggle with fear, self-image, confidence, and self-worth. Through faith-centered reflections and practical spiritual insights, it offers hope and encouragement while guiding you toward lasting inner healing.

Overcoming Obstacles includes fourteen devotionals that can be used daily or weekly as a foundational guide. While not a comprehensive manual on inner healing, it shares personal insights that help Christian believers discover their identity in God, shift their perspective, and grow emotionally and spiritually.

This is an invitation to reflect, heal, and move forward with faith.

Are you ready to confront what's holding you back and begin the journey toward wholeness?

BOOKS BY TERRYANN SCOTT

Hidden Truths: Daily Devotional

Hidden Truths is a powerful daily devotional that equips Christian believers with spiritual wisdom, biblical discernment, and eye-opening insights rooted in God's Word. In a world where deception often disguises itself as light, this devotional helps expose the subtle and hidden works of the enemy while pointing readers back to the unchanging truth of Scripture.

Discernment is a vital part of the believer's walk with Christ. The Bible warns that not everything that appears good is truly from God, and that even the devil can present himself as an angel of light. Hidden Truths encourages readers to test every spirit, grow in spiritual awareness, and guard their hearts against deception through prayer, reflection, and biblical truth.

Each devotional is thoughtfully written to be educational, thought-provoking, and spiritually awakening, stirring the believer's heart toward a deeper, more intimate relationship with God. While not exhaustive, this devotional offers personal insights and practical spiritual reflections to help Christians grow in knowledge, faith, and spiritual maturity.

Perfect for daily reading, Hidden Truths invites readers to pause, meditate, and pray after each entry—creating space to hear God more clearly, strengthen discernment, and discover Him in a fresh and meaningful way.

Ideal for:

- Christians seeking spiritual growth
- Believers desiring deeper discernment
- Daily devotional and prayer time
- Personal reflection or small group study

Finding God: Love Devotional

Finding God is about pursuing Him. It is about going after God with all your heart and discovering Him, especially in hard times. God is almost always discovered through pain, based on the individual's response to the challenge, and pain can therefore be a blessing in disguise when used to draw near to God.

I discovered God through much heartache and pain (I spoke about this in *The Revelation of the Dragon: No More Walls, vol. 1*). *I remember when I thought my life was over and that* the only person I had left was God. This caused me to experience a rude awakening, which brought me closer to Him. I was a Christian for many years, but it was not until I found Him in such a profound way that I realized I was like Peter, walking with God, but not converted.

After my conversion, I noticed that things changed

dramatically with only a little prayer and sincere effort on my part, as I focused on God and put His Word into practice. I was amazed at how much I discovered God, so much so that I decided to marry my newfound lifestyle with much prayer. That was when I found it is not just in the praying, but in the doing. There are many men and women of prayer whose lives remain the same because they are hearers of the Word and not doers.

My eyes were immediately opened as I discovered the seriousness of living out the Word of God in obedience and merging that lifestyle with prayer. I got astounding results with little prayer and by becoming a doer of the Word, rather than just a hearer, compared to much prayer and no results due to a lack of practicality. What we do is more important to God than what we pray and how long we pray. God honors our lifestyle and obedience above our prayers.

God is a practical God, and if you need results, follow me for a few days on this journey throughout our Love devotional guide. Are you ready to discover His presence?

BOOKS BY TERRYANN SCOTT

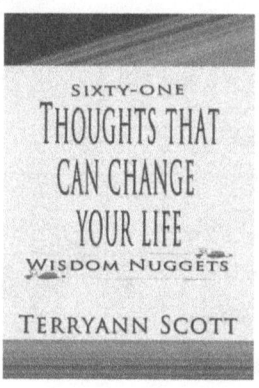

Sixty-One Thoughts That Can Change Your Life: Wisdom Nuggets

One thought can shift your perspective. Sixty-one can transform your life.

This book is a personal compilation of sixty-one powerful spiritual thoughts drawn from deep reflection, prayer, and meditation on the Word of God.

Each thought is designed to inspire clarity, strengthen faith, and invite meaningful change through intentional application in everyday life. These reflections are not theoretical—they are practical, faith-centered insights meant to be lived.

When embraced and applied, they encourage spiritual growth, renewed thinking, and a deeper connection with God.

Whether read slowly for reflection or revisited during moments of prayer and study, these spiritual thoughts serve as gentle reminders of God's truth, purpose, and transformative power.

If you are seeking encouragement, spiritual insight, and a renewed mindset rooted in Scripture, this collection offers timeless wisdom to help guide your daily walk of faith and positively shape your life—one thought at a time.

BOOKS BY TERRYANN SCOTT

* * *

BOOKS BY TERRYANN SCOTT

* * *

"To the only wise God our Saviour, be glory and majesty, dominion and power, both now and forever, Amen" (Jude 1:25).

www.ingramcontent.com/pod-product-compliance
Lightning Source LLC
Chambersburg PA
CBHW031401040426
42444CB00005B/376